CONTENTS

SECTION 1

PREPARING FOR THE LAB -------- 4

SECTION 2

WORKING SAFELY ------------------ 8

SECTION 3

HANDLING ACCIDENTS------------16

SECTION 4

CLEANING UP ------------------------ 24

More about science safety and Max Axiom...................28–29
Glossary..30
Find out more..31
Index...32

KT-162-978

Dr Khan?

Hi, Max. I'm testing a sticky lolly mixture.

I have to stay here and watch it heat up. We never leave a heat source unattended.

I'm testing different flavours to see how higher heat affects each one.

149° C

ANISE VANILLA MAPLE

Just like Dr Khan, we're using glass beakers to heat our water and chocolate.

But porcelain or metal containers can be used to heat substances as well.

Whatever container is used, it should have a label that says "heat resistant".

HEAT RESISTANT

Looks like your water is ready for the next step in this experiment.

Professor Axiom!

Uh-oh. I better see what's going on over there.

Quick, dude, clean it up!

Wait just a minute! We need to treat all spills in the lab the same, whether it's a chemical or something as harmless as water. And I'll bet the hot plate is still hot, isn't it?

Yes, it's still on and plugged in.

All right. Proceed carefully because an electric shock is possible if you touch a wet appliance that's still on.

Not to mention the danger of all this broken glass.

Am I speaking to the caretaker?

Yes.

We could use your help in Mrs Williams' science lab.

So why can't I just unplug the hot plate?

Because electricity and water don't mix. Water conducts electricity. If you unplug an electric lead with wet hands, you may get electrocuted.

QUICK FACT:

The human body is mostly water. So your body conducts electricity. That's why you must be careful around electric appliances.

Look at Dr Khan.

Her work station is tidy and dry. If she ever spills something, it is cleaned up right away. That's a safe place to conduct science.

When using knives, you have to be careful when cutting or chopping something in the lab.

Let me demonstrate how sharp this knife is on a strand of Billy's hair.

PLOINK!

Hey!

Well done for cutting away from your hands. That's proper cutting technique.

COLD

HOT

SCIENCE SAFETY

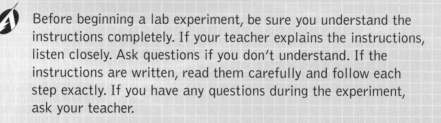

Before beginning a lab experiment, be sure you understand the instructions completely. If your teacher explains the instructions, listen closely. Ask questions if you don't understand. If the instructions are written, read them carefully and follow each step exactly. If you have any questions during the experiment, ask your teacher.

They may not be fashionable, but safety goggles must be worn at all times in the lab. For the best protection, use goggles that shield your eyes from both chemical splashes and flying objects. These goggles are always labelled with the code ANSI Z87.1.

Right now your body has more germs on it than there are people living in the United States! Washing your hands for at least 20 seconds is the best way to prevent millions of germs from passing to your mouth, nose, and eyes.

Environmental scientists test soil and water for pollutants. In 1989, the *Exxon Valdez* crashed and spilled oil into Prince William Sound, Alaska. Wearing protective clothing, environmental scientists helped determine the best cleanup methods. With their help, the area is slowly returning to a healthy environment.

Learning about animals is fun, but handle lab animals only if your teacher gives you permission. If a lab animal bites or scratches you, be sure to tell your teacher immediately. Also, wash your hands before and after you handle an animal. Washing hands protects you from passing germs to or receiving germs from the animal.

Scientists use safety equipment for the type of science they are doing. Scientists studying erupting volcanoes sometimes wear silver full-body suits. These suits have a metal coating that reflects the intense heat of molten lava. Scientists studying sharks sometimes wear shark suits when diving. These suits are made of a steel mesh that protects against shark bites.

 Some protective gloves are made of latex. This material can cause an allergic reaction in some people. If you experience a rash or itching while wearing latex gloves, tell your teacher.

MORE ABOUT

SUPER SCIENTIST

Real name: Maxwell Axiom
Height: 1.86 m (6 ft 1 in.)
Weight: 87 kg (13 st. 10 lb.)
Eyes: Brown   Hair: None

Super capabilities: Super intelligence; able to shrink to the size of an atom; sunglasses give X-ray vision; lab coat allows for travel through time and space.

Origin: Since birth, Max Axiom seemed destined for greatness. His mother, a marine biologist, taught her son about the mysteries of the sea. His father, a nuclear physicist and volunteer park warden, showed Max the wonders of the earth and sky.

One day, while Max was hiking in the hills, a megacharged lightning bolt struck him with blinding fury. When he awoke, he discovered a new-found energy and set out to learn as much about science as possible. He travelled the globe studying every aspect of the subjecct. Then he was ready to share his knowledge and new identity with the world. He had become Max Axiom, Super Scientist.

GLOSSARY

allergic reaction sneezing, watery eyes, swelling, or rashes caused by contact with plants, animals, or substances

biohazard biological agent, such as blood or body fluids, that may carry infectious diseases

biologist scientist who studies living things

chemist scientist who studies or works with chemicals

contaminated dirty or unfit for use

corrosive able to destroy or eat away at something little by little

flammable can burn

germs small living things that cause disease. Bacteria and viruses are two common types of germs.

habitat the place and natural conditions where an animal lives

latex a milky liquid that comes from certain plants. Latex is used to make rubber.

poisonous able to kill or harm if swallowed, inhaled, or touched

porcelain a hard ceramic made by firing and glazing clay

sharps knives, needles, and broken glass

specimen a sample that a scientist studies closely

FIND OUT MORE

Books

Has a Cow Saved Your Life?: Scientific Enquiry, Deborah Underwood (Raintree, 2007)

Scientists at Work series (Heinemann Library, 2008)

Tabletop Scientist series, Steve Parker (Heinemann Library, 2005)

Team Projects, Barbara Somervill (Heinemann Library, 2009)

Watch Out!: Science Tools and Safety (How to Be a Scientist series), Susan Glass (Heinemann Library, 2007)

Websites

http://www.tryscience.org/

Go to the Try Science website and have a go at some fun experiments. Remember the safety principles you've read about in this book.

http://www.bbc.co.uk/schools/podsmission

Click on the "Electricity" button for Annie's fun activity. Read Ollo's safety tips, then try Pod's experiment.

INDEX

accidents, 6, 8, 16–23, 26
    broken glass, 16, 18
    burns, 21
    fires, 20, 21, 22
    spills, 6, 16
allergies, 12, 29
animals, 13, 28
asking questions, 5, 28

beakers, 10, 14, 15
biological materials,
    12–13, 28

chemicals, 10–11, 16, 25, 28
cleaning up, 24–25

electricity, 16, 17, 20
emergencies, 5, 23
exits, 23
experiments, 5, 8, 10, 11, 12,
    13, 14, 15, 24, 27, 28

food and beverages, 8–9
fumes, 11

germs, 6, 7, 9, 12, 26, 28

hazardous symbols, 25
heat resistant containers, 15
hot plates, 14–15, 16, 17, 21

instructions, 5, 8, 10, 14,
    27, 28

knives, 19

labelling containers, 11
lab waste, 24–25

pollutants, 12, 28
protective clothing, 6–7, 8,
    12, 28, 29

rules, 5

safety equipment
    aprons, 6
    eye wash stations, 22
    fire blankets, 22
    fire extinguishers, 20, 22
    first aid kits, 23
    gloves, 6, 23, 29
    goggles, 6, 28
sharps, 18–19, 25
stop, drop, and roll, 21

wafting, 11
washing hands, 26, 28
work stations, 8–9, 17